Live Free Facilitator's Guide

A Guide To Empowering Live Free Curriculum Participants

By Harmony Dust, MSW

Live Free Facilitator's Guide
A Guide To Empowering Live Free Curriculum Participants

Harmony Dust
PO Box 5311
Sherman Oaks, CA 91413
info@iamatreasure.com
www.iamatreasure.com

Cover Design by Moonwalker Digital
Interior Design by Moonwalker Digital
Illustration by Moonwalker Digital

Published by Treasures Ministries 501 (c) (3)

Paperback ISBN: 978-0-9863338-7-3

First Edition

Ordering Information:
Special discounts are available for large quantity purchases. Please contact the publisher by email: info@iamatreasure.com or visit www.iamatreasure.com for more details.

Printed in the United States.

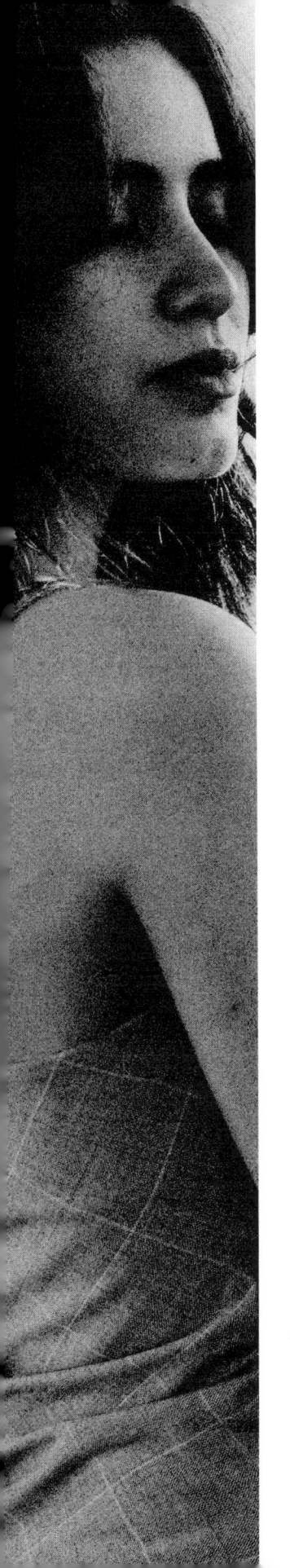

Table of Contents

Welcome!

The mere fact that you have this guide in your hands brings me great hope. It was someone like you, a person with a desire to empower me to breakthrough and LIVE FREE, that became the catalyst for incredible transformation in my life. She wasn't a licensed clinician or the director of a non-profit. In fact, she was just a college student with empathy and a heart that loved unconditionally. Her friendship changed my life. She was a confident woman with healthy boundaries, determination to pursue her dreams and a faith that was tangible. Within a year of meeting her, I gained the courage to leave my pimp and walk away from a life of exploitation in strip clubs.

I know the power of the one. One person can make a difference in the life of one person... who can then make a difference in the life of another one.

This guide is designed to help you be that *one* for someone.

As you set out to support Live Free Curriculum Participants, this facilitator's guide will equip you to understand:

• The role you will play
• The impact of complex sexual trauma
• The core concepts of the curriculum, including Stages of Change and The 7C's of Resilience
• How to facilitate curriculum-based discussions with Live Free participants, both one-on-one and in support group settings

THE IMPACT OF COMPLEX SEXUAL TRAUMA

Before we dive into the principles of the Live Free Curriculum and the unique role you will play in supporting participants, it is important to recognize the effects of complex sexual trauma and the unique challenges participants may be facing.

The more we understand the way sexual exploitation and trafficking impact people's lives, the better equipped we will be to support them on their journey to freedom and healing.

I know firsthand that sexual trauma can have profound and long-lasting effects on a person's life. I have personally navigated many of the challenges listed below. It is important to acknowledge that everyone's story is different and everyone responds to trauma differently.

With that said, here are some common threads we see:

THE IMPACT OF SEXUAL TRAUMA

1. Psychological and Emotional Effects: Sexual trauma often leads to a range of psychological and emotional responses such as post-traumatic stress disorder (PTSD), anxiety, depression, fear, shame, guilt, and anger. Survivors may experience flashbacks, nightmares, and intrusive thoughts related to the traumatic event, which can disrupt daily life and overall well-being.

2. Relationship Difficulties: Sexual trauma can significantly affect one's ability to form and maintain healthy relationships. Survivors may struggle with trust, intimacy, and establishing boundaries. They may have difficulties with emotional and physical intimacy, or experience challenges in developing and maintaining healthy relationships.

3. Self-esteem and Self-worth Issues: Sexual trauma can profoundly impact an individual's self-esteem and self-worth. Survivors may blame themselves for the trauma or feel a sense of shame and guilt. They may struggle with feelings of worthlessness, self-doubt, and negative body image.

4. Sexual Functioning and Body Image: Sexual trauma can affect an individual's sexual functioning and overall relationship with their body.

5. Substance Abuse and Self-destructive Behaviors: Some survivors may turn to substance abuse or engage in self-destructive behaviors as a way to cope with the overwhelming emotions and psychological distress caused by the trauma. These behaviors can further complicate their recovery and overall well-being.

6. Physical Health Consequences: Sexual trauma can also have physical health consequences. Survivors may experience chronic pain, somatic symptoms, gastrointestinal issues, sleep disturbances, and other stress-related physical health problems.

THE IMPACT OF SEXUAL EXPLOITATION AND TRAFFICKING

Sexual exploitation and sex trafficking are specific and complex forms of sexual trauma that have their own additional and distinct ways of impacting survivors. Here are some ways in which sex trafficking can impact survivors differently:

01 COMPLEX TRAUMA:

Sex trafficking survivors commonly experience what is known as complex trauma. This refers to repeated and chronic exposure to traumatic events over an extended period, often involving multiple perpetrators and situations. Complex trauma can lead to more severe symptoms of PTSD, difficulties in regulating emotions and behavior, and a higher risk of developing dissociative disorders.

02 LOSS OF AUTONOMY AND CONTROL

Survivors of sex trafficking often experience a profound loss of autonomy and control over their own bodies and lives. They may be forced into engaging in acts against their will, subjected to degrading and humiliating treatment, and

have limited or no ability to make choices about their own bodies and boundaries. This loss of control can have long-lasting effects on survivors' sense of agency and self-empowerment.

03 STIGMATIZATION AND SHAME:

Survivors of sex trafficking may face heightened stigmatization. Society's perception of trafficking survivors can be influenced by stereotypes and victim-blaming attitudes, which can exacerbate feelings of shame, guilt, and self-blame. This can make it even more challenging for survivors to seek support and disclose their experiences.

04 COMPLEX NEEDS:

Survivors of sex trafficking often have complex needs that require specialized support. These needs may include health care, trauma-informed mental health services, assistance with housing and employment, legal support, and help reintegrating into society. Addressing these complex needs requires a comprehensive and multidisciplinary approach.

O5 POTENTIAL FOR RE-TRAUMATIZATION:

Survivors of sex trafficking may face ongoing threats from their traffickers or be at risk of re-exploitation. They may also encounter difficulties in finding safe and stable environments after escaping or being rescued from trafficking situations. These factors can contribute to a heightened risk of re-traumatization, which can further impact their recovery and well-being.

Supporting survivors requires a trauma-informed and survivor-centered approach, including access to specialized services, comprehensive care, and the recognition of their unique experiences and needs.

If that list above is overwhelming to you, join the club!
I overcame much of what was mentioned and it can still feel a bit staggering to me to see it all named like that.

Here is the good news!

With appropriate support and resources, survivors can work towards healing, reclaiming their lives, and building resilience. And YOU can play a vital role in empowering them to do just that!

ABOUT THE LIVE FREE CURRICULUM

The Live Free Curriculum is a series designed to equip and empower women who have experienced sexual exploitation and trafficking to live healthy and flourishing lives.

Free To Thrive is the first of several volumes to be released in this curriculum.

The entire curriculum has been created with two key principles in mind:

1. Stages of Change
2. The 7C's of Resilience

STAGES OF CHANGE[11]

Stages of Change is a model created to help us better understand the (often messy) process of change. It can also help us assess an individual's readiness to move towards a new and healthier behavior so we can best support them.

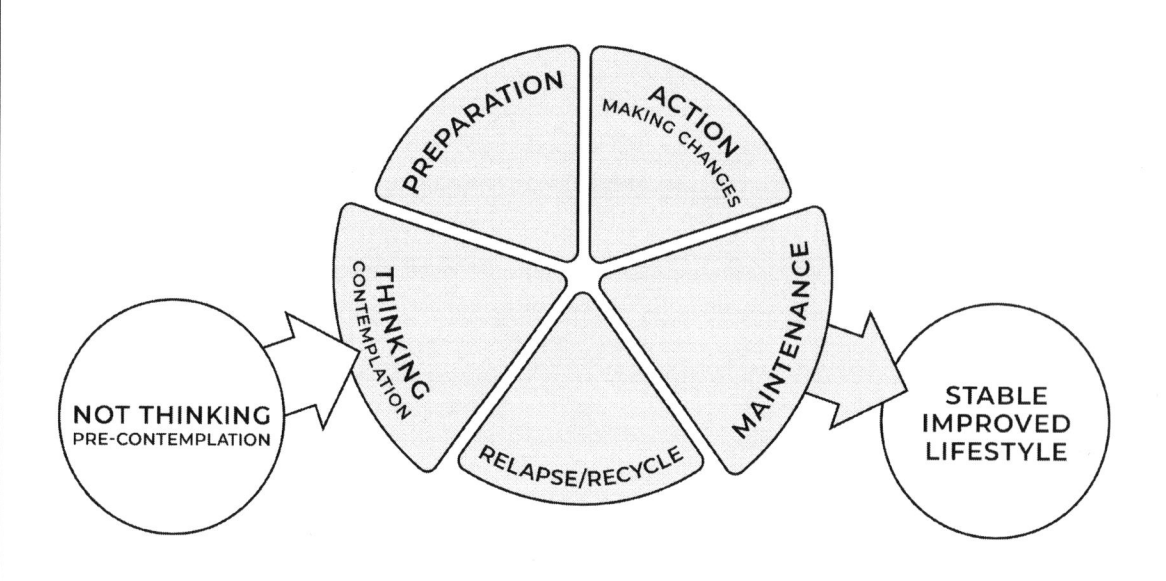

[11]Prochaska, JO; Norcross, JC; DiClemente, CC. Changing for good: the revolutionary program that explains the six stages of changeand teaches you how to free yourself from bad habits. New York: W. Morrow; 1994.ISBN 0-688-11263-3.

THE 6 STAGES OF CHANGE ARE AS FOLLOWS:

Stage 1: Precontemplation (Not Ready)
The first stage in the Stages of Change Model is Precontemplation. When we are at this stage, we aren't really thinking about changing. We do not intend to start the healthy behavior in the near future (within 6 months) and may even be unaware of the need to change.

Stage 2: Contemplation (Getting Ready)
In the Contemplation stage, we are getting ready to change. We are thinking about change and intend to start the healthy behavior within the next 6 months. We probably still have a lot of mixed feelings about change (also known as ambivalence), which might make us want to keep putting it off.

Stage 3: Preparation (Ready)
When we are in the Preparation stage, we are ready to start taking action within the next 30 days. We take small steps that we believe can help us make the healthy behavior a part of our lives. For example, we tell our friends and family that we want to change our behavior.

Stage 4: Action
When we are in the Action stage, we have changed our behavior within the last 6 months and need to work hard to keep moving ahead. In this stage, it is normal to think about going back to old relationships and habits. With the proper tools and support, we can keep moving forward.

Stage 5: Maintenance

We are in the maintenance stage when we have changed our behavior more than 6 months ago. We are likely aware of the situations/people that may tempt us to slip back into unhealthy behaviors and relationships.

With newfound healthy coping skills and a good support system, we will be empowered to stay the course.

Stage 6: Relapse/Recycling

In addition to the stages above, the researchers identified the concept of Relapse or Recycling. Relapse/Recycling is not a stage in itself, but it is the return from Action or Maintenance to an earlier stage.

It is important to note that this is a normal part of the process of change for many people and does not mean that they cannot continue to move forward.

As you consider the person or people you intended to support, it will be helpful to determine what stage of change they are currently in.

FREE TO THRIVE CURRICULUM

Free to Thrive is Volume 1 of the *Live Free* Curriculum. While the *Free To Thrive* workbook can be helpful to people in every stage of change, it is specifically designed for those in precontemplation or contemplation. It is intended to be a gentle invitation to build a more robust support system, a stronger sense of self efficacy and begin to explore the idea of change. Our goal is to inspire participants to tap into their hopes and dreams and begin to imagine a life free from sexual exploitation and trafficking.

COMING SOON!
In the future, we will be launching the next few volumes of the *Live Free* Curriculum. Each volume will be designed for participants in the progressive stages of Stages of Change.

Free to Heal (Volume 2), will equip participants in the Preparation and Action stages of Stages of Change with the tools they need to engage in recovery and solidify their decision to live free.

RESILIENCE

I am constantly in awe of the resilience of the human spirit. Our capacity to recover from the pain and difficulties life seems to dish out so plentifully is truly astounding. Many of the women who inspire me the most have been through unthinkable trauma, and yet, they remain standing, with miraculously tender hearts, a fierce determination to encourage others and a desire to leave the world a better place. To sum it up, they are resilient.

Pediatrician and human development expert, Kenneth Ginsburg, M.D. suggests that there are 7 building blocks that make up resilience, known as the 7 C's of resilience.

The 7 C's of Resilience

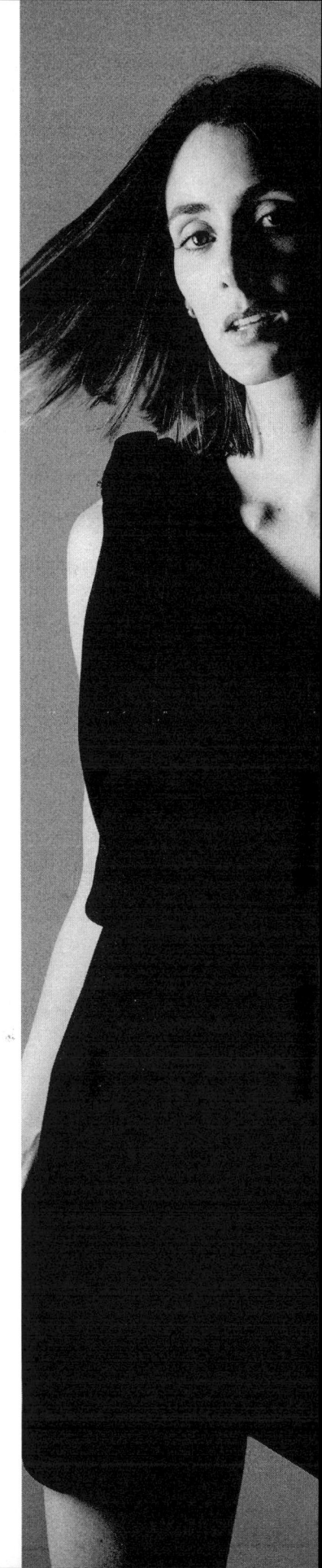

01 COMPETENCE
the ability to handle situations effectively

02 CONFIDENCE
the belief in one's abilities or capabilities

03 CONNECTION
a sense of closeness with/attachment to
people and community

04 CHARACTER
a fundamental sense of right and wrong
that enables us to stick to our values

05 CONTRIBUTION
a sense that we can make the world a
better place through our contributions

06 COPING
our capacity to manage and respond to stress

07 CONTROL
the belief that we have the ability to make
choices that will impact outcomes in our lives

Resilience is key to a thriving life. Because resilience is so vital to our ability to rebound and recover, each section of the workbook is developed to help foster a specific area of resilience.

SUPPORT GROUPS

At Treasures, we have found support groups to be powerful spaces that inspire incredible growth and healing. Each volume of the *Live Free Curriculum* can be used to facilitate support groups. In the next section, I will share some tips on how to use *Live Free* to facilitate discussions in a support group setting.

In the meantime, I thought it would be beneficial to share some important support group guidelines that we have found helpful in creating a safe and supportive atmosphere in our groups. We read these guidelines outloud at the beginning of each new season and anytime we have a new support group participant.

SUPPORT GROUP GUIDELINES

1. KEEP YOUR SHARING FOCUSED ON YOUR OWN THOUGHTS AND FEELINGS

Focusing on yourself will benefit your recovery as well as the ones around you. Stick to "I" or "me" statements, not "you" or "we" statements. Avoid going into detail about what other people did or said, and instead focus on how their behavior has impacted you.

2. PLEASE LIMIT SHARING TO THE ALLOTTED TIME

We want to ensure that everyone has a chance to share and that one person does not dominate the group sharing time. If there is time at the end of the group, anyone who has more to share will be given an opportunity to do so.

3. NO CROSS-TALK PLEASE

Cross-talk is when two people engage in conversation via talking or chatting in the Zoom messenger excluding all others, making distracting comments or questions while someone is sharing, speaking to another member of the group while someone is sharing, or responding to what someone has shared during his or her time of sharing. Each person is free to express her feelings without interruptions.

4. WE ARE HERE TO SUPPORT ONE ANOTHER, NOT FIX ONE ANOTHER

We do not give advice, try to solve someone's problem, or offer book or counseling referrals even in our own time of sharing. Input on someone's share is only welcome when it is asked for.

5. WHAT IS SHARED IN THE GROUP STAYS IN THE GROUP

Anonymity and confidentiality are basic requirements. This also means not discussing what is shared in the group among group members. This is called gossip. The only exception is when someone threatens to harm themselves or others. Please be advised, if anyone threatens to hurt themselves or others, the group leader has the responsibility to report it.

6. DURING SHARING, WE WILL REMAIN SENSITIVE & ATTENTIVE TO THE NEEDS OF OTHERS

We ask that you avoid sharing graphic details. If you need to process the specifics of your trauma/experiences, we encourage you to speak with a mentor or therapist. If anyone is triggered by the content of someone else's share, it is important that the person being triggered lets the group know. From that point, the conversation will either be altered to keep the group safe for all members and/or the person being triggered will have the option to talk about it.

7. SUPPORT GROUP MEMBERS ARE EXPECTED TO ATTEND DRUG & ALCOHOL-FREE

Attending under the influence interferes with group member's participation, their ability to recall material covered, and the ability of other group members to benefit from the session. Engaging in recovery work with a sober mind is vital.

8. WE AGREE TO PRACTICE HEALTHY CONFLICT RESOLUTION

If we have an issue with someone (including leadership or staff), we will approach that person directly, with respect and kindness. We will not vent our frustrations to other group members or ask them to take up our offense. If you need support in navigating an issue, we encourage you to speak to a staff member or mentor privately to find solutions. For the well-being of the group, if you find yourself emotionally escalating during group, we ask that you engage in grounding techniques to remain calm. If you need additional support to get grounded, you may step outside with a group leader.

9. PLEASE NO PHONES DURING GROUP

Though we're in a virtual group, please silence and put away cell phones during group time. This allows the group to be respectful and focus on what each person says.

10. WE WILL RESPECT GROUP MEMBERS RELIGIOUS/ SPIRITUAL BELIEFS

Though Treasures is a faith-based organization, we do not require anyone to ascribe to a certain set of beliefs and will respect the beliefs of others.

***FOR ONLINE GROUPS

11. WE AGREE TO FOLLOW ONLINE SAFETY AND ETIQUETTE

To prioritize confidentiality and safety within the online support group we ask that you join in a safe private space with the camera on, where the screen is only visible to you. Please wear headphones when necessary to protect the confidentiality of everyone in the group. If something comes up and you need to leave your screen or move around we ask that you message the support group co-leader to let them know that you will be turning off your camera. Additionally, outside recording devices are not allowed to capture the session.

FACILITATING DISCUSSION

Whether you are providing care to an individual going through this workbook or leading groups of people through it at once, here are some suggested questions to help you facilitate meaningful discussion.

If you are doing an 8-10 week support group, you may want to consider...

- Combining a couple of sections for discussion purposes each week
- Select the sections of the workbook you believe would be most valuable to discuss in your group.

SAMPLE DISCUSSION PROMPTS

• What did you learn about yourself as you completed the last section you worked on?

• Was there anything that felt hard about the section you just completed?

• What was your favorite question or activity and why?

• How do you think the topic in this section can help you grow or thrive in life?

You may also want to use one or more of the reflection questions in the workbook to facilitate discussions on a particular section.

THE ROLE YOU WILL PLAY

By choosing to support those who have experienced exploitation and trafficking, you have potential to make a profound and lasting impact on their lives.

Here are some empowering thoughts to guide you on this transformative journey:

1. Safe Space:
You possess the incredible ability to create a safe and supportive space for survivors to heal and grow. Your presence and willingness to listen without judgment can be a powerful catalyst for their recovery. Your empathy and understanding can help them regain trust in others and in themselves.

2. LifeLine:
By forming a meaningful connection with survivors, you offer them a lifeline of support. Your presence can be a beacon of hope, reminding them that they are not alone in their journey. Your belief in their potential can ignite their own belief in themselves, instilling them with the courage to overcome their past experiences.

3. Inspire Empowerment and Agency:

You have the opportunity to empower survivors to reclaim their autonomy and sense of agency. You can encourage them to make choices, set goals, and take steps towards achieving their dreams. You can help them recognize their strengths and talents, reminding them that they can make powerful choices that will shape their own lives.

4. Foster Resilience and Self-Compassion:

Many of us have often endured immense hardship, but we are not defined by our past. You can support survivors in cultivating resilience by providing a safe space to explore their emotions, process their trauma, and develop coping mechanisms. You can encourage self-compassion and remind them that healing is a journey with ups and downs.

As you are faithful to show up for "the one" it has the potential to create a ripple effect of positive change, breaking the cycle of trauma and empowering survivors to embrace their full potential. Your dedication and belief in their capacity to heal and grow can inspire them to become advocates, mentors, and sources of strength for others.

As you support others on their journey to Live Free, may you bear witness to the resilience of the human spirit and our incredible capacity to not only overcome trauma, but also to see it transformed into a legacy of hope and ultimately, freedom.

ADDITIONAL RESOURCES

Available at: **www.iamatreasure.com**

SCARS AND STILETTOS

At thirteen, after being abandoned by her mother one summer and left to take care of her younger brother, Harmony becomes susceptible to a relationship that turns out to be toxic, abusive, and ultimately exploitative. She eventually finds herself working in a strip club at the age of nineteen, and her boyfriend becomes her pimp, controlling her every move and taking all of her money. Ultimately, she discovers a path to freedom and a whole new life.

SOMEONE I LOVE

In this short, interactive guide, you'll learn how to support your loved one when they are engaged in harmful patterns, behaviors, and relationships. No matter how deep in despair your loved one may be, there is hope. And you have an opportunity to play a vital role in their journey to freedom. This interactive guide will show you how!

TREASURES ONLINE TRAINING

Want to help women in the sex industry and survivors of trafficking find lasting freedom and healing? Treasures Training is for you if you want to...

· Effectively support women in the sex industry and survivors of trafficking
· Better understand trauma and exploitation
· Start a strip-club ministry or outreach

YOU CAN MAKE AN IMPACT.
WE'LL SHOW YOU HOW.

Since 2007, we have trained hundreds of leaders, including members of the FBI, DOJ, social workers, law enforcement, churches and NGOs world-wide. Now in digital form, our training is more accessible than ever to you and your volunteer team.

Included in the training
· 6+ hours of video training
· Treasures Training manual
· Quiz questions to ensure understanding
· Sample documents
· Support Group Guidelines
· Outreach Training (Only Outreach and Care Track)
· Volunteer Training (Only Outreach and Care Track)
· "Should Prostitution be Legal" Bonus Video
· "Sex Sells" Bonus Video

To learn more or enroll, visit:
https://www.iamatreasure.com/trainingso

Notes

Notes

Notes

Notes

Notes

Notes

Notes

Notes

Notes

Notes

Notes